Everything Is Fine

Stephanie Chestnut

BookLeaf
Publishing

Presentation by *BookLeaf Publishing*

Web: www.bookleafpub.com

E-mail: info@bookleafpub.com

ISBN: 978-93-95950-60-2

First edition 2022

Hold on John.

ACKNOWLEDGEMENT

I acknowledge myself for continuing to try.

PREFACE

The letters strung together in this book are those of experience. Relation to experience and the reactions of a highly sensitive person. May cause risk to an already confused mind.

Glimmer.

A certain year ago, I broke into an inconceivable
expanse.
Withal, new pieces emerge on the ground where
I walk today.
Wary to no more chisel lines into my skin,
I explore the crystalline fragments delicately.
Amidst wonder and remorse,
I fail to recall where they once belonged,
But with recognition, they once had a place,
Suddenly infinity is possible.

As If Time

As if you were here yesterday.
As if I ever experienced you at all.
I feel you slipping, too shy to ever fully bask in
your glory.
Tender new freedom when the less you know
keeps you fresh,
and the things yet to come,
keep you awake.

Suppression

It's scary to allow the swell,
After giving up so many times.
Fool me once.
I exist in the mirage of self.
If I give into the craving of betterment,
the drop from an ivory tower so greater than
slithering into sand.

A Day in The Life

Reckless seas; one thousand, four hundred, and
thirty. Count the half penny, you'll need it.
I'm begging you on my knees. Holiday on
mute.

   no I don't want to talk to you.

   "Sorry I missed your call", it's been a while
since I've been able to press the button.

   If only things were a little bit different.
Pinched neck nerve, textured skin, endowed
youth, is it real? The sky pa rt s late in the
day, revealing summer blues in the middle of
winter. I can convince myself it's different time
of year;

     perhaps even one you were in.
Summer haze, no it's a winters blaze, what
happens when I have nothing left to say?

Around the Corner

5

You come up a lot, all grey and fake.

Newness

July born feet walking freshly cut grass,
too curious not to waddle towards strangers,
oh little man you have so much life ahead of
you.
Welcome to the Global World,
on your first self-lead exploration through the
park,
acquiring unique natural artifacts,
specifically selected off the ground,
ordinary novelty still beautiful,
I wonder how it is to wander with such ease,
try not to forget.

Unwanted Expansion

In heat, condensation dripping down iced tea,
constant jittering of the fan now nothing but
white noise against the swell.

My feet resemble that of a woman in labor, my
body aches, pains, and cramps and try's to make
room for the fullness.

Spelling

why open the door to another with the last still
ajar?
begging a new endeavor with thee,
while I still dream of … he.
O & T, the sequel to S & G,
raking up the letters on my jacket,
the one I lost in the laundry,
which of the alphabet will come next?
((turns out it was - JR. – from the future))
departing at random,
after I divulge and indulge,
wading in the scent of skin.
I miss them, all of them, in small ways,
I would allow in,
to render me weak and believing in the heavens,
weight of the letters so sweet,
leaving yearning to be. alone.

Behind Gabbing

I speak of boys but if you know the truth I am burning in my own flesh and drinking poison to swelter the pain.

Destruction is a form of Creation.

God made the sun,
God looked at the sun,
God destroyed the sun.
I found truth in your eyes,
Until you closed them.

it was nice

Havoc runs rampant on the brick-laid roof,
innate thumbs twist together the unspoken
words,
small-handed rain pattering to the sound music,
echo's of nature from your tape player,   (of
course you have a tape player)
echoing of past and future.
If we are present, where have you been?

Inside

Staying small, in the smallest room of the most
minuscule house in a pocket-sized town,
carpeted in vines, in the tinniest corner,
scrunched up in a ball, fetal as the day you were
born, holding your breath, hands over your ears,
shutting your eyes tight, gulping down Alice's
drink me potion, ripping through flesh, gnawing
off your fingertips, stunted into petrifaction,
where nobody will ever find you.

Over there...

13

In the water
   In the water
 I'm in the water.

Tasting Silver with Red

I explored alone,
cool metal intense as he,
like Joan of Arc,
withstand the pain that came,
full of naked oozing indentations,
Baby-deer,
forbidden, and I drank.
I'd gone too far,
I lived for a while,
under nowhere with my primal experiment,
I'd lost time.
Motive for displaying my bruises; it's obvious.
To flush toxins,
dirty, bloody, wet;
the texture, the colour,
made me vomit,
rushes to heal,
bathe in amethyst,
petals drifting past gardens,

the tiny wounds,

I try not
to never talk again.

Honesty

Flashbacks in hues of mixed messages,
self-doubt, and loss,
the shape of your teeth ripping through,
cut your head off with words,
to make you feel the most you've ever felt.
Snapping grown bones between pinky fingers,
your mouth dropping slightly to the left,
kind eyes by definition,
behind them, only you knew.

I Take it Back

16

Grace did not drip from my fingertips this morning as I was too busy weeping over chiseling's gone wrong. Flung back sediment settled behind my pupils, already widened from the previous night's events when things got taken too far.

SPRINGTIME

Hand-painted Easter eggs under plastic Jesus'
gaze,
on your knees weeping to Him while the fresh
breeze wisps,
caressing the pussy…
willows outside.
one lucky groundhog and one lucky bunny
pulled from a lab in the spirit of
Mother Nature as she wishes us a new with
drizzling flowers and longer days,
too bad we usually feel more inclined to kill
ourselves in the rain.
I plucked at green clovers to bring to your home,
they only have three leaves each,
luck, a favour rarely given,
but I just couldn't leave the park without,
something to brush over your gouge.

Change is the Marker of Time

leave one shoe tilted,
winter gloves and a sundress,
the one time I really needed you my fingers
dented,
sore and bruised detecting distance.
what a perfect time for your re-arrival,
grey, most likely seventy years old,
walking the silver lining,
    "What's behind the gate?"
    "That's where we're going."

Ism's

The seven-foot-tall
holy grail of
a drunken haze.

I was cynical
by-the-glass.
arm flung back - out of my spine - overindulge,
those are qualities we share.

fresh silhouettes,
built using sand,
gently cleanses,
murky wine.

How Many Times?

Incomplete portrait standing tall, shaking, like a
leaf against the breeze,
 bracing for the blow,
after blow, after blow, after blow, after blow,
after blow, after blow, after blow, after blow,
after blow, after blow, after blow, after blow,
after blow, after blow, after blow, after blow,
after blow, after blow, after blow, after blow,
after blow, after blow, after blow, after blow,
after blow, after blow, after blow, after blow,
after blow, after blow, after blow, after blow,
after blow, after blow, after blow, after blow,
after blow, after blow, after blow, after blow,
after blow, after blow, after blow, after blow,
after blow, after blow, after blow, after blow,
 cont'd.

Until the Next

Hey, look at that! it's the last one!
There is "Something" where there once was
"Nothing",
    willpower is a finite resource.
but that's okay, in fact it's just fine.